GHOST GEAR

GHOST GEAR

Poems by Andrew McFadyen-Ketchum

The University of Arkansas Press
FAYETTEVILLE • 2014

Copyright © 2014 by The University of Arkansas Press

All rights reserved

Manufactured in the United States of America

ISBN-10: 1-55728-654-X

ISBN-13: 978-1-55728-654-3

18　17　16　15　14　　5　4　3　2　1

Text design by Ellen Beeler

♾ The paper used in this publication meets the minimum requirements of the American National Standard for Permanence of Paper for Printed Library Materials Z39.48-1984.

Library of Congress Control Number: 2013956225

For Lisa

To begin, darkness.
            —Neil Gaiman

There was a double bed, a mirror,
a double bed in the mirror . . .
                    —Vladimir Nabokov

Everywhere I look I see fire; that which
isn't flint is tinder, and the whole world
sparks and flames.
                    —Annie Dillard

Acknowledgments

Grateful acknowledgment is made to the journals and anthologies where these poems first appeared or will soon appear: "The Torchbearer," *Anti-*; "Singing," *Ascent*; "Perseus," *Bellingham Review*; "Constellations," "Tonight," *Blueline Review*; "First Catch," *Cimarron Review*; "Lost Creek Cave," "Sacrament," *Connotations Press*; "Ghost Gear," *Copper Nickel*; "For the Return of God," "Nightswim," *Cutthroat*; "Golden Paper Wasp," *Eclipse*; "The Ever-Chamber," *Fifth Wednesday Journal*; "The Word Damn and the Word God," *New Letters*; "Night Driving," *Poet Lore*; "Stormdraining," "The Year Hyakatuke Was Said," *Poetry Sucks: An Anthology of Poetry, Music, and All Sorts of Bad Language*; "Slag," *Potomac Review*; "Winters We Watch Snow Descend Slowly," *South Dakota Review*; "Corridor, "Meditation on Balsam Mountain," *Southern Indiana Review*; "Corridor," "Driving into the Cumberland," *The Southern Poetry Anthology*; "The Lives of Boys," "Self-Portrait at 5 A.M.," *Spoon River Poetry Review*; "Singing," *What Matters?*

Endless thanks to my teachers, mentors, colleagues, and friends whose criticism, encouragement, and wisdom has shown me the way: Newell and Tasha Anderson, Brian Barker, Nicky Beer, Helena Bell, Mark Brewin, Brian Brodeur, Bill Brown, Jason Lee Brown, Tony Colaianne, Kerry James Evans, Ed Falco, John Flaherty, Malcolm Glass, Peter Grimes, Nathan Hansen and the Hansen Family, Jeff Hardin, Georganne Harmon, Rachel Hawley, Andrew Hudgins, John, Beth, and the Interlandi clan, Jake Kelly, James Kimbrell, Barry Kitterman, Sandy Longhorn, Beth Lordan and Andrew Curtis, Jean McGraw, Krystal McMillen, Travis Mossotti, Simone Muench, Kenneth Northington, Gregory Pardlo, Pamela Parker, Rick Pechous, Mike Pilola, Donald Platt, Jamie Poissant, Leonard Scigaj, Tim Seibles, Amie Whittemore Shea and Tim Shea, Dave Smith, Joyce Sommer, Katherine "Bonnie" Soniat, Jason Tabeling, Joan Thomas, Jon Tribble, Dennis Welch, Peter Wyatt, Jake Adam York, D. Gilson, Aaron Wheetley, and Peter Wyatt.

Special thanks to the following for reading this book and telling me how it is: Jenna Bazzell, Martin Call, David J. Daniels, Kurtis Hessel,

Matthew Huff, Alexander Lumans, Rodney Jones, Allison Joseph, Keith Montesano, Ed Pavlic, Joshua Robbins, Jeffrey Schultz, and Robert Wrigley.

Judy Jordan, this book wouldn't exist without you.

I owe a debt of gratitude to Serenity Gerbman and Emily Booth Masters of the Tennessee Young Writers' Workshop; Ron Mitchell and the RopeWalk Writers Retreat; the BearLodge Writers and the Devils Tower National Monument Writer's Residency; and the Blue Ridge Writers' Conference for their support.

Thank you Enid Shomer for selecting this book and for making it better. Thank you to the folks at the University of Arkansas Press for making such a beautiful book. Thank you Siolo Thompson for the incredible cover art. And thank you to Dana Gioia, T. R. Hummer, and Paisley Rekdal for your kind words.

Thank you to my parents, Steve and Linda McFadyen-Ketchum, my sister, Elizabeth M-K Sullivan, and Billie and David Schlueter for your support.

And, finally, Lisa. Thank you for everything. Every poem here is yours.

Contents

Singing 3

MY FATHER SAYS YES

Tonight 7

Ghost Gear 8

Sacrament 12

Constellations 14

The Ever-Chamber 15

Winters, We Watch Snow Descend Slowly 18

Golden Paper Wasp 19

SUMMER OF GODDAMNS

Meditation on Balsam Mountain 25

The Word Damn and the Word God 26

Stormdraining 29

For the Return of God 31

Slag 32

The Torchbearer 36

The Lives of Boys 38

Night Driving 40

CORRIDOR

Corridor 45

The Year Hyakatuke Was Said 47

Driving into the Cumberland 50

Self-Portrait at 5 A.M. 52

Nightswim 53

Perseus 55

Lost Creek Cave 56

First Catch 63

GHOST GEAR

SINGING

What do I know of God but that each winter
I thank him for it? No spider webs
snagged in the bluestem, no horseflies at rest
in blossoming cones of henbit, no slug trails penned
to the cooled hoods of cars. We are creatures all,
stillborn to the language of split pine rails
standing in their pickets, ice glazed to bone
in every rut, the stealth tracks of jays a sleepless
ideography in the snow. But we are not
entirely alone between the mountain ranges,
in these hours condemned to darkness
before the sun gyres open the face of February
and the red flare of Mars grows dim.
Just outside my door, the burr oak is wintered
full of grackles—hundreds of coin-
eyed scuttles ornamenting its branches. Here,
my breath plumes gray. In the distance,
brush catches fire. The wind, if you watch,
is calligraphy; the stars in winter,
a weightlessness. The grackles are doors,
rasping their flight plans limb to limb.
The grackles are doors, some limned with light,
others black. Rising, my arms have long
been open. Stepping across these thresholds,
I step across these thresholds. Singing, I sing.

MY FATHER SAYS YES

TONIGHT

April 17, 2007

Tonight, the sun gutters down to its wick as daylight
strains and refracts in skirls across the lake's wide water.

Heavy rollers of rain heave against headland and tree line.
Lightning falls in its slow white script to farmland
                                  and watershed.

Still, I know so little of the rain that plays this lake
like a snare—time run thin through the sky's turnstiles,
all the grief and shrift I cannot hold but do
                                  moving in from the north.

What else can I say of these ball-peen hammers
of distant thunderheads? What else can I say
of this lake most deep where the mud newt sups
and the black leech dreams of swimmers and blood?

If only I could drop into sediment and murk, so much lost
of the heart's heave through amnion and the liquid wake
and sleep, so much forgotten of the ocean's collapse
and the skull cap's crowning. The boom. The crux.
The good steel bolt slid home in the flame.

Here, in these first few minutes of dusk, I say *Sunset,*
you take too much—sun having preened
its glossy spoke, last light departed into the west.

Here, tonight, I say *Land, you leave us too soon*—
sky bottomed out, the lake clicked shut.

GHOST GEAR

Low tide, my father highsteps the trammel net, stoops
half-submerged in Tanaga Bay and begins the work
of disentangling another sockeye from the interlaced snares.

He stands before me now, the same foot shorter
he's been the last ten years, my sister and I
nothing back then but a notion
when my father could hold his breath

well over a minute,

how or why I've learned not to ask, the familiar arc of his story
cast out like he, the newest member of the crew,
flung to the farthest edge of the intertidal.

I could hear better then, he adds.

Good thing, I always think. Otherwise,
he'd not have heard that thin cry of alarum from the beach. Otherwise,
he'd not have looked up from his work

to see the bellowing cord of the continental shelf
rise to obscure summer's first dusk as if Britomartis herself—
goddess of fishermen—has half-risen from the sea
to encompass that final island of the Aleutians.

Dumbstruck, my father watches the wave suck in the tide
like a maw: his legs, Wranglers rolled to the knee,
for the first time exposed, the net an organism in and of itself,
a bare root system, salmon left clapping wet sand

as far as the eye can see
                    a wave the width of his vision charging the land.

My father claims that in such moments,

        the body lightens.

My father claims that there, he saw himself
bird's-eye view, that he watched himself look up at the sky
and the sky had become a mirror.

        And he sees his body ascend the cumulus
as if pulled by threads of light, each thrust of the sky's wide wings
lifting him ever closer to a rift in the clouds.

        But my father does not kneel genuflect to the gods,
my father does not consider his sins or ask for forgiveness. Rather,
he gives his marrow to those ropes,
he weaves himself into those moorings.

        And the last thing he sees is the wave.
And the last thing he hears is something like the clap of a thousand hands.

And the sea took him.

Language fails my father here, so he resorts to sound:

        Wham!

slamming one open palm into the other as if to quash
something living, his posture surging in our living room—
the tumblings of his cliffhanger—
body whipped by the imagined sea.

How do I describe what seemed like hours beneath the waves?

I am a poet retelling a telling.

The sea did not care about my father,

       But

the wave came and went and my father
held his ground, the backdraft strong in the wave's wake—
Britomartis' final tug for his spirit.

And he lashed the flesh of his life from that ocean.

And the water receded.

Now, my father lights up when he tells how he returned to the beach

       as slowly as possible

and how, when the men finally saw him emerge from the sea,
they cheered his name, my father returned
from what they believed to be the dead:

       Ghost gear, they call it:

nets and riggings lost at sea to fish for no man.
Blindly trolling seines illuminating the deep
with their bioluminescent catch.
Ruptured buoys and trammels coasting past coral reefs
until they drift down,

       down into the dark.

Only once have I asked my father
why he chose out there to live. Only once
has he told me that as the wave approached,

        he heard a voice.

And that voice asked him,

     Are you a father?

And my father said,

   Yes.

SACRAMENT

You claim this is your earliest memory: the day
they brought me home, head matted with doll's hair, eyes

puckered against the light of the new world—you,
my sister, and they, our mother and father,

baptized in the weeks following birth, touched,
they say, by mercy. Unforgiven, I tutored myself in the ways

of sacrament, slipping through neighbors' windows,
curious which gods or devils would rise

from the basement foundations, or palming
from our father's dresser the .22 rifle rounds

I claw-hammered open to powder the bomb that panged
the tree-frogged dark into silence. Perhaps

it was sleeplessness, perhaps it was the romance of streetlights:
folding my nightclothes neatly on the bed, I slinked alley

to alley, a pale specter just visible beyond the oak-line.
Now, just home for the holidays, when my breath mists

my bedroom window, a fog blossoms across the garden
wild with sumac and turkey claw grass—this the story

of my beginning, that fabled heat radiating down
from the July sun, a snicker of sunlight between the bodies

of my makers—this the story of my conception
and I seeking some way to tell it. So why not

somewhere down in the garden by the alley we grew up on?
Why not our mother and father coupling

in a row of tasseled corn, the human fires
rising between them? When we talk about my first days,

you remember you refused to leave my side,
curled beneath my crib like a nautilus

sent singing from the waves to rock me in the arms
of my first earthly sleep. If only I could sing

the songs you sang to me then. If only I could sing
them here, twisting in the iridescent turns

of the Siamese fighting fish in its scummed fishbowl.
O sister of earth, O sister of night, let's stay awhile,

roosted in this hereplace deep in the body of our makers.
O sister of vesper, O sister of shadow, I still believe

it was you who instructed me in the ways of waiting
to be born, you who told me Child, fear not, harsh truths

are first translated into whispers. You who said Child, call out
if ever you are lost and we will call back, so I dropped,

wailing as I came from the house of all souls.

CONSTELLATIONS

Outside, children snag fireflies in the fallow field,
return home, cupped hands lighthouses of flight,
countless brilliant lantern-heads surrounded by bone.

Later, caged in a mason jar set before the window,
the bronze disk of its lid slipped open for air, a handful
of fireflies lie folded beneath a single blade of grass

as night's storm angles in through the curtains,
their glass apocalyptic speckled with random bulbs of rain,
each flickering streetlamp multiplied and shimmering

as the flies try again to ignite their pyres,
constellations descended, these echoes of fire.

THE EVER-CHAMBER

Here, the earth with its own compositions:
   the *wheep-wheep-wheeps* of the American avocet,
mirror-waters flushed by red-eared turtles,
   wind humming the black willow woodwinds,
trumpet creepers' siren song.

Here in the realm of the swamp where light
   is anything but still and my father's mother warned him
Never enter, each whisper of his machete
   promises the city of conquistadors
paved with gold cobblestones, rivers of liquid ivory,
   Ponce de León and his crew aged not a day.

Here, Shreveport, Louisiana, 1958, where instead of glory
   he finds the cottonmouth hung like tinsel
with the violet blooms of sharp-winged monkey flower,
   warming its blood by those few rays of sun
that finger through the willows, my father approaching
   with grand sweeps of his blade.

   Imagine that moment for the serpent,

he says, its sudden wakened eye black as a poppy seed,
   then that banded machinery of scales,
the clap of its jaw unhinged to action.

   Gravity holds little dominion over the dedicated body

and it's almost comical the way my father mimes
   the way the snake struck, reaching slow motion
with his left arm, two fingers transformed into fangs, his eyes

15

and mouth growing into large Os
    as he twists away from the strike, right arm swinging down
just in time through the air

that here, in our living room—
    another Christmas Eve, another birthday—
is nothing more than air
    but in that swamp became a flickering:

the reels of his future spinning before him
    like wartime clips of men dropped toward France,
their parachutes iridescent jellyfish in the night.

There, in the swamp, he saw Vietnam
    as though from the pages of an atlas:

serpentine coastline of the South China Sea,
    a row of bodies lined up along a dirt road,
draft card a declaration of flame in his grasp,
    disappointment inscribed across his father's face.

There, between my father and the snake:
    a dreamy image of the day my sister would bolt
out the back door and he'd search the neighborhood
    for hours, fearful he's lost her;

two years later to the A.M. of my birth, body purple
    with meconium and blood, the screams of this child
for once welcome, skull warped with labor, gauzy
    as a milkweed's seed pod.

    The swamp will show you things.

Then the machete and cottonmouth met,
    and the snake split in half, the blood of it splayed

in meticulous streams of black, the flat medallion of the wound
  like a plastic model of the cell: a nucleus of bone
surrounded by nerves, tissue, and chaos.

Here he stands. Still. Shocked he cannot reverse
  what he's done. *Stop!* his mind had ordered. But here
the mind holds little over fate.

Here, had he stepped miles back with his left foot
  rather than his right
as he entered the sway of black willows,

he'd be the one clutching at his struck face, virus
  tunneling the chambers of his mind,
swamp waters rising,

and it would be the cottonmouth seeking another tree trunk
  settled in the waters, certain in the ever-chambers
of its mind of what it's done, certain

as the gold-domed cells of black willows,
  as the *kuk-kuk-kuks* of herring gulls,
my father thinking of his mother

who'd only taught him the little she knew
  as he turns to hack that snake into its smallest parts,
the ink of it spreading across the water's surface.

Retreating, he matches each footstep that brought him here,
  and when he emerges from this waving,
unbalanced world, the hard-packed earth of the non-swamp
  holds everything higher so that when he looks toward the sun,

the barn swallows dip lower, spread their wings
  to catch some air, then rise again, bobbing like buoys
along the invisible thread of their passage through the sky.

WINTERS, WE WATCH SNOW DESCEND SLOWLY

as pear tree blossoms, white bloom
after white bloom tumbling down in arcs
to melt back into water on the tip of the tongue.

Children, night after night on the floodplain
fall backward in the drifts, arms spread wide
as gull's wings opened to the sea breeze

then fanning like moths, flashlights
tracing ellipticals as if to conjure spirits
from the haloed wash of earth.

Who am I to tell them no gods will emerge from this sky
drawn flat by clouds, the light of the town adrift
above the trees like the white of an eye?

Who am I to tell them soon their mothers
will call them in and all that will be left
are these scanner beams of taillights, red tracers in the distance,

this field of winged bodies edged out of snow,
a field of negative space, this plot of land just steps
from my back door a plot of unmarked graves

where I watch the warm sockets of homes click shut
one by one, waiting for the child-self to appear,
stuffed in the winter coat that should be hanging limp

on its nail in the hallway as he moves from grave
to grave, hands linked together at the thumbs like birds
to mimic our flight into the redshift?

GOLDEN PAPER WASP

Now it's Emma May's porch that I remember,
and the knock-kneed skirt hems of the girls
who swung on the porch swing, the birch-
white columns solid as live pines, the wind
chimes strummed by angels I believed
secreted themselves in the eaves. And how,
when that golden paper wasp fell from the sky
and landed on my ear, everything froze
as though one of my winged imaginings
had ascended the sun-flashing heavens
and streaked backward against the revolution
of the clocks: trees no longer moved by wind,
cars passing by in gold blurs, the screech
of the girls' swinging scudded to a halt
by the bleached-white tips of their Keds—
that wasp at rest in the fleshy cradle of my ear.

That's how it came back: the memory
of that afternoon Chris and I practiced long bombs
between the double doors of his root cellar
and our end zone drawn between the peach tree
with its single, sad globe of fruit and the Chevy
S-10 on its throne of cinderblock and switchgrass.
Then, I had no idea what a mining bee was
but learned when, leaping, I snagged
yet another spiral single-handed from the sky
and, landing, heard what later I'd be told
was the crunch of my foot in their hive,
that matrix of spit, larvae, and roots
we'd observed their laboring over all summer

and from which they bore upward so fast
that by the time I'd sent that football
spinning on its nose like a top
on the asphalt of the alley, was engulfed
by a whirling vortex of wings and stings.

A year later I was still known as the kid
who tried outrunning a swarm, dashing headlong
from state-named street to state-
named street. I missed three weeks of school
with a fever and when I started to feel better
would leap before my bedroom window,
the other kids in the neighborhood
playing scared as they ran from our yard,
screaming news of the creature that lived
in the house on the corner of 52nd Ave. and Park.

But there on the porch, I froze,
stock still and wide eyed while the wasp
foraged the fine hairs of my auricle like a bloom.
And I was lucky to be looking west
when that flash-green split of the sun
unscrolled across the horizon and night,
yet again, held its domain. Still,
it seems logical to think of the lunar module
my mother watched rise from the surface
of the moon when I envision how that wasp
must have looked when it lifted a wing
and lifted from my ear—this long before
I understood why my mother told me never
take a ride with Mike LeFleur, my baseball
coach who always smelled of ham hocks
and nickel wine, or why I shivered
when the men who prowled our streets

in station wagons and coupes
rolled down their windows, reached
out a hand, whispered, *Come.*

But I knew what it meant the day I turned sixteen
and one of those girls from the porch asked me
to take her for a drive. She didn't tell me where
she wanted to go but knew the way,
and when we got to the local swimming hole
and she slipped her skirt from her hips
on the edge of a sandbar, I followed
the thin trace of her body without a sound.
These days, when my wife starts from sleep,
it's usually the sound of our house
gathering itself against such quiet. For me
it's the phantom whine of the wasp
as it works its way deeper down the tunnel
of my ear. For me, it's anything that lost
making its way through the dark.

SUMMER OF GODDAMNS

MEDITATION ON BALSAM MOUNTAIN

for Mary Interlandi, 1983–2003

The stars are so numerous tonight, I've nearly lost myself
connecting them: Virgo barely risen from the heat-weak
horizon, the great bear all but invisible against its milky smear.

Somewhere below these loci of brilliant light, somewhere
beyond the earth's backward bow, there's a certainty and silence
to be found, a purpose and answered prayer. Yet, when the sun

reappears, the barred owls will be wise to halt their questioning,
the mountain lions will catch a scent they dare not follow.
If I knew the way to the life of such wild things, I'd go there:

the evergreens' constant shift, a razor-edged escarpment
through a pass, wings banging against the moon. But no matter
how many times I dream of not waking, I do. No matter

how many times I rehearse the proper words, they all
but spill from my mouth. *Come, show me the way,*
I demand of Polaris's burning heart. *Come*

finish what you started, I mouth to nothing and no one,
yet again having counted the stars on this bald peak,
yet another unnamed and nameless hour ticking into the next.

THE WORD DAMN AND THE WORD GOD

Who knows what strung those words together on my tongue
the summer Chris moved in across the alley, all those long
June hours we tiptoed the rusted-out railroad, begging

for the vibration of approaching freight or playing Yahtzee
camped out in the dome tent pitched in his backyard,
searching in the numbers for any sign of first light.

But my money's on the afternoon I stepped into a mining bees'

hive, mid-stride catching a touchdown spiral with time running
out, their home woven among the roots of Chris's peach tree.
For weeks thereafter, St. Ann's across the street called *Repent!*

Repent! I the kid who stormed the neighborhood in escape
of bees, crying countless curses, every inch of my body scorched,
a hymnal of Goddamns tucked between bicep and bird chest.

Chris's father poured two gallons of gasoline on that construct

of whispers, and my father let me watch him drop a lit match
into the earth from our high kitchen window. That night
Chris gave me a mason jar of dead miners curled up

like wolf spiders swept out from under the couch, and all night
I dreamt of the mason's magic, bees rising on invisible spindles
in the grass in that pause between time and conflagration.

But my mother decided it was Chris, who through the darkness

of a few nights later she heard screaming Goddamns
with each strike of the father's leather across the son's back.
I cried when my father told me I no longer could play with Chris,

and he wept when I said, *But Chris is all I have.* Chris
who caught a carp a day later, his prize strung up by an arm's-
thick tree branch through its breathers. Chris

who liked to strum the testicles of his pit bull Rex,

mean as hell kept chained to a sycamore by the alley
between our yards but when Chris was around turned
into the sweetest thing. Chris who I thought of this morning

as fog lifted to reveal three acres of wheat grass frosted silver
reaching for the polestar like a bed of nails, and I was flung back
to the day I stumbled from Chris's basement with a two-by-four

rust-nailed to my heel—Chris unhooking Rex's chain,

the panic bitter in my mouth, my eyes squeezed shut,
then the warm slap of Rex's tongue from foot to nail, from nail
to foot—Chris and I bearing witness to the healing power

of a dog's saliva as he rubbed Rex's balls and Rex groaned
as blood eased from my skin. He and his father moved late
that fall, chasing factories Deep South, and now Chris lives

in that place where everything seems true. Some say his father

took to Evan Williams. Some say Chris simply became
what he already was. And I wish I could say I've run into him
in line at the DMV or at some bar I've come to for the dancing

and there's Chris stitched into fishnets, neon strobes like moons
in his vinyl knee-highs, eye-shadow thick as clay in tire tread.
Wish I could say we've laughed over beers and told old stories,

slapped one another on the back and argued over the tab.

But Chris's father didn't bother to clean the boning knife
sequined from yet another Sunday on Arkabutla Lake,
three largemouth reserved on their bed of ice,

Rex outside howling. And now I wonder if this explains
that Summer of Goddamns Chris yowled down all those dreary railroad
miles, how he always knew at the splits which curves turned

toward the switchyard and which paved the path

to Tennessee's Jerusalem. So *glory be* to the Goddamns
he cried all those hours it takes a knife to the gut to kill a man.
Goddamns to the hours it must have taken Chris to die.

Goddamns to the carp we never caught, to the knife
destined for Chris's gut. Goddamns to all dogs too weak
to loose their chains. Goddamns to all the stories we do not tell.

To all fathers angry with their sons,
                              Goddamn.

If I could, I'd take Chris in my arms. I'd get down with the grit
and linoleum and patch that rift of skin with my tongue.
I'd hold the boy drunk between two lives.

I'd freeze ourselves and wait for the sculptor
who fools greatness out of stone, our two bodies draped
one into the other.

    The word damn and the word God.

STORMDRAINING

That summer we grew tired of the mammoth carp of Richland Creek,
  the trash fish who lulled in the deep, warm runoff of that tributary

and who rose—open mouthed, wide eyed—for our lures
  like the souls of the forgiven before turning mockingly back over

to flash their brilliant bellies in the sun. When Tim's preacher
  told him carp didn't eat worms, *only duckweed,* that bioluminescent

cloud cover that couldn't be strung *on even God's tiniest hook,*
  he and Sam started talking all the more about the storm drain

not a mile upstream, the storm drain that fed the creek with its perfect
  rectangular mouth, the storm drain said to reach *as far as Niggertown.*

We spent our hours after summer school constructing our raft
  of scrap wood and bald tires, stockpiled flashlights and rubber waders,

canvassing the neighborhood each eve for the gallon Purity jugs
  we strapped like pontoons to the keel of our marauder. My father

must have overheard our talk the day he emerged from his work
  to tell me, *Son, nigger's not a word you use in my house,*

but when I tried convincing Tim of this, Tim only looked up
  from hammering a roofing nail, said, *Niggertown*

is Niggertown, and that was that. All August we searched
  those angular viaducts of night, like spelunkers in God's

most perfect cave, grave robbers tunneling toward the unknown dead,
  each excursion venturing us further beyond the point

where the pearled tubes of our flashlights faded as Tim and Sam
  recounted tales they'd heard their fathers tell of Niggers

and Aunt Jemimas to pass the time. I kept quiet about my father
  who'd marched in Little Rock, my father who kept the death threat

rubber-banded to the brick pitched through his dorm window in 1966,
  our journey measured every quarter mile by the rays of sunlight

that hovered, ghost-like, beneath the street grates and my companions
  who waded into the still, flat water to boost me to the steel I gripped,

searching for names on street signs or addresses on mailboxes,
  any indication of where beneath our world we were.

Eventually, Tim and Sam grew tired of those days of undiscovery,
  of the decision left, right, or straight at the junctures, our voices

echoing the unlit fathoms: *Hello, hello, hello . . . Where are we, where are we,*
  where are we . . . Who, who, who . . . And it was all I could do but listen

to the mad splashes of abandonment the day Tim and Sam took off
  with the raft as I hung from a high grate, slatted by bars of daylight,

their cackling slowly receding. I have no idea how long I hung there.
  .I don't remember Tim or Sam's last names. But I do know

I hung long enough to watch daylight fade and for the stars to appear.
  And there was the calm that came with finally letting go—a flash

of weightlessness and the drop of all pressure.
  And the waiting that followed. And the night. And the dark.

FOR THE RETURN OF GOD

The day He invented the universe, God gathered
His museum of stones in a mason jar
and cast it to the cold star of oblivion.

When the boy would come home from school, nose bloodied
from yet another fist swung up from out of nowhere,
he'd borrow that jar from the cupboard, swipe
the river stones and split geode that lined
his mother's vanity, clack his sister's string of pearls
along the edge of her jewelry box, snag
the ghost-white marble from his father's collection
stashed like a secret in a shoebox on a high office shelf.

In the backyard, the boy would uncork the jar,
sweep those gems wide around him. Geode the sun.
River stones, nine planets. Marble: moon. Those pearls
a ring of galaxies holding hands in tight circle around it all.

Then he'd wait. First for the stones to shudder,
then levitate. To form a swirling vortex
in the air and slowly corkscrew back into the jar
with a sound like wind through trees.

He'd wait for the jar's lid to screw itself back on.
Then pop. Seal. He'd hold the jar in his hands
and shake it like a rattle, listen to the hollow clatter of stars,
earth, and everything else he couldn't comprehend
clinking like punched-out molars between rows of teeth.

For a long time he waited for the return of God.
For a long time, the wind stayed very, very still.

SLAG

I remember sweat, three pennies pressed wide
by the twin track of the train
barely a cinder's heat in my pocket, shirt slicked
to my back like the last bit of flesh on a picked-clean bone.

    * * *

Long and hard I've worked to forget those weeks
before the school bell's toll and summer slipped its closed sign
over like a red burn across the horizon.

So why address that August
Leo and the Virgin set such slow pace across the hemisphere
and the Stanley brothers organized the neighborhood's
Huffys, hallooing like Pawnee over the crests of every back-alley
I knew, bareback and hungry for my dirty-blond scalp?

Why tunnel back along the grooved slate of memory?
Well over a decade since I crouched siphoning nectar
from the orange clappers of the honeysuckle patch,
starved and too scared to follow my own trail back
along the runged straightaway of the rail
and down the trestle's nearly unclimbable slope—
                                               sun

not yet gone under, moon still waiting
to cast its lukewarm light long across the road.

It's no great leap into the folds of the wings of the crows,
to perch with them on the power lines, red eyes open
then closed, and all the time myself within that aperture,

just having discovered the abandoned repair yard, moon
double Dutch in the crow-trussed cable wires.

* * *

Is it the gadfly born with a thousand black blind eyes?
The goldfish that lives without a single memory?
The pit viper that strikes without ever having heard a sound?

Make me one.

For if anything's worth recalling, I'd not have thought
of this plain of shimmering glass shatterings beneath the sun,
the power lines converging and diverging overhead
like a cat's cradle twined between sassafras branches.

* * *

Long and hard I've worked to forget, fingered
the folds of the hops blossom for the dander of forgetfulness,
tossed this husked-out volume of a body
to the fruit bats pinging out a flight from darkness.

But no roots have sprouted from the cold stone floors.
No sweet herb of amnesia has curled up from the guano.
No cornflower blue blossom in the deep.

* * *

Make me a goldfish, and I'll leap out of water.
Make me a viper, and I'll strike at my own wings.

For it is here, under this near-full sphere
gray as a bingo ball, I wiled my hours, scouring
busted-up Budweiser bottles and crushed cans
of Milwaukee's Best for globules of slag,

that intimate byproduct of butane's blue cone
left long ago by spot welders to cool
into the egg-shaped stones I gathered
and, reaching back, heaved into the sky,

believing that like the men who strapped themselves to Apollo
and rocketed beyond gravity's grasp,

I too could shuttle past the caws of the crows,
leave my booted foot's impression on the surface of the moon.

      * * *

Then the moon seemed so close,
pinned to the earth like angels to the dead,
moon like a sand dollar revolving about its axis,
                                  so thin

that every half-turn it winks out,
leaving only the dark slit of a serpent's eye closed over us.

      * * *

Is it the pickerel reed that snaps
in the first cool breath of autumn?

Is it the seven-year cicada that discards its husk
on the cusp of winter?

      Make me one.

For what else is there for me here? Other
than the rust-rimmed railings left out to their half-lives, other
than the typefaced destinations fading along the sterns
and starboards of de-wheeled hopper cars,
the crows passing their messages back and forth between them,
the crows my cackling overseers?

* * *

Make me a piece of the sky, and I will darken.
Make me a crow and, as darkness falls, I will make myself
a part of it.

How else forget these first notions of self-loathing,
that no matter how hard I tried to send something into orbit,
those lumps of molten iron pitched, yawed,
then splashed back down to earth
in thumped-up instances of light?

How else forget the path that brought me there or how,
looking back along that wide curve in the rail,
I wished for the galloping forth of the Minotaur,

and instead it was the Tennessee Southern barreling forth
the coal economy as I crouched just inches
from the flashing-past boxcars,
envisioning the day I'd take off at a sprint
and hurl myself into another land.

THE TORCHBEARER

If you ask, my father will tell you
       the story of building his first
crystal radio: night after night

       after lights-out, a sheet draped
like a mosquito net across his bed,
       shadow creatures cast

across the slapdash walls of his tent
       as he worked: first, a pair of hands
flapping before candlelight,

       then a V of snow geese towing
the floral print northward,
       finally, a school of fish

frantic within a paper lantern.
       If you ask, my father will tell you
when he finally finished constructing

       that radio, he stumbled upon a voice
who told the story of a traveler
       and the world he discovered uninhabited

by light, its people blind as cave
       pool fishes. When he tells the story
of that night, he never fails to mention

       that though he pinched himself awake,
he fell asleep never having heard
       the story's end and became in his dream

the explorer landed on a planet
　　　　cloaked in darkness. And in the darkness?
A rustling of creatures in the brush.

　　　　The call of a child in her sleep. A star
overhead, eclipsed and dangerous cold.
　　　　Sometimes, before he thought

me old enough, I'd ask my father
　　　　what made the solar system. He'd tell me
God gathered stones in a pickling jar

　　　　and thrust it to the cold nucleus
of the elements, our great obsidian
　　　　peppered with dust. Sometimes,

when I close my eyes, I can almost see him
　　　　in search through the night for that voice,
fingers delicately maneuvering the tuner's knob,

　　　　the crystal's black longitude
sliding east to west its brief radio range.
　　　　But all he ever finds is static

and the morning with no sleep.
　　　　All his adult life he's waited
for the turn of the page that will send

　　　　him back to that sightless world,
eyes torches, hands turned to flame,
　　　　the vestigial sockets of the desperate

glowering forth from the pitch,
　　　　my father the first torchbearer

to surface in ages, my father the mystery
　　　　between fire and flame.

THE LIVES OF BOYS

Your lives have no end, we were told, because
    they've not yet started, our names the blank expanse
between birthdates and extinctions that papered
        our classroom walls: Chris Clausen who wrapped
        his hands in gauze for weeks after closing them
    .around the bright red nose of a bottle rocket

or Sam Smith who snuck warm, off-white cans
    of Olympia beer from his father's stash,
answering anyone who called him a drunkard
        with his fists, and Satyr Grimes and Edward
        and Tim, his brothers, who lit a spare Goodyear
on fire behind the closed doors

of the Shell service station, lucky to return
    from St. Thomas a few weeks later—ears gnarled
to dog's chew toys, strange interruptions
        in their speech. But it was I who first vaulted
        the sagged chain link that barred the way
    onto Old White Bridge, ignoring the signs of NO

TRESPASSING, tired of leaping stone
    to stone across Richland Creek. Picking our way
between unpatched cracks in the macadam,
        it no longer mattered what movies spun
        on their reels at the Lion's Head or what candies
    we'd select from the concession stand's poor box

of light, only the trail we blazed below the thrum
    of traffic east and west in the shadow of the new bridge,

38

the tang of vomit and whiskey drifting up
    with the snap of rapids from the creek below
   where we skipped rocks across the backs of bluegill
and called out in response to the rusty incantations

of grackles. It was only a matter of time
    until Chris ventured out onto the two-by-four
that bridged the gap in the eastbound lane where, one by one,
    we tested ourselves, board warping back
    and forth, the world seemingly gone quiet
as we spread our arms for balance—Old

White Bridge yet another threshold our mothers bade
   do not cross though our fathers knew we would anyway.
And it was Sam who was first to break, concerned,
    he claimed, our flirtations with chance
   would make us late for the film. We punched Sam hard
in the shoulder for flinching the two-mile trek

to the theater and all throughout the movie,
   drinking noisily from our sodas and ignoring
the turned heads of shooshes until Sharon Stone
    uncrossed her legs and silenced us all.
    Not a one of us knew what we'd witnessed,
on our way there or somewhere below

that projector's ray of flickering frames.
   At any moment, Old White Bridge could have flung us
into a darkness where no one would make out
    our row of open-mouthed faces—
   nothing quite like the heat that simmers up
around the lives of boys, the red world extant

behind the eager, unblinking eye.

NIGHT DRIVING

How many nights did our neighbors
at the halfway house gather to watch me,
barely thirteen, half in and half out
as I pushed my mother's Toyota Corolla
beyond the hill's grip to pick up speed
on the downslope until, just out of earshot,
I'd pop the clutch and ignite the night
with a single spark? Odometer
unplugged. Speed dial a broken reed.
Nashville. Spring, winter, fall, summer.
The hour late. The air mostly still.
Sometimes damp or cold. Always dark.

Some nights I cruised downtown,
humming the sounds that tumbled
from the Dixie-swing dance floors.
Others, I took a left turn off Broad
and drove west along the shipyards
of the Cumberland where Peterbilts
and turbochargers idled with their payloads
of coal still smoldering with the pressure
of creation on the barges that bobbed
on the waterfront. Moving south,
I rose high above the city
where the reservoir mirrored the sky
in its ashen sheen. Sometimes
I wandered deep into the numerous
districts of brick-house tenements
not a mile from my home, the impoverished
pooled on street corners, silver

crosses hung around their necks,
their red-and-white swooped sneakers
flashing beneath streetlamps.

But it was the US-70 that jarred me
from sleep, the vague path of its vapor trail
that shot me past the county line
and into farmlands stacked between cold
trout streams and hay bale lanes.
There, I tested speed and gear-
to-gear ratios. There I learned I *could drive*
beneath the boughs heavy with blossoms
or with their bareness. And it was
a right turn, a thin trail, and the drum
of packed gravel and drainpipes
I passed over that took me to the center
of a soybean field—the horizon
a blue and milky curve like the white
backbone of a bluebird's feather,
Cassiopeia lurching beyond the swerve
of bats on the hunt, the white
points of gnats blinking out. And I could feel
myself drift open. And I saw the gossamer
spines of a dandelion head, then the wheat
of my own brown hair. Puffs
of exhaust from my mother's car.
Green curlicues of the pubescent field.
A bend in the Cumberland
and the patchy skew-work of farmland.
Then a plane's cold metal
pressed through me, and the earth
dropped from its fallopian tube,
hanging in space like a spider's egg
before a window of night.

I never left that place. I never
returned to that place. And every night,
I told myself, would be the last.
But every night the night beckoned
and there was nothing quite like the luster
of first light, often copper or peach,
one time: scalp white. Later,
old enough, I'd teach friends how to peel out:
left foot pressed hard to the clutch,
right foot hovering—that trick
I learned on my last night drive,
three blocks from home, sixteen
a weekend away. Revving my engine
I enticed a Taurus into a race,
and when the light turned green, fishtailed
twenty-five feet of rubber and oil
down Charlotte Avenue.
When I looked in the rearview,
I saw the wisps of ghosts, the peel
of their pursuit deafening.
When I looked where I was going,
there gleamed the dual red eyes
of my demons so far ahead
I thought I'd never catch up.

CORRIDOR

CORRIDOR

Drunk, we wound our way up the wind-bent
stilts that loomed above the old Marathon
Building, abandoned in the days long after
our father's fathers milled cotton and women
bobbed their hair, each step skyward reporting
in the hollow iron we ascended. From there
the world swayed with the wind and our tinny echo,
our legs hung out over the lip of the city, scissor
kicking at the night. From there we could cradle
that city in our hands as big rigs and V-6s swung by
on the S-curves of I-40, a pair of spotlights
probing figure eights in the clouds over downtown,
the projects rehearsing their somber tunes
of rebuilt Chevy Novas and catcalls and bass.
Now, when I return home, I pass that water tower.
During the day, it just stands there. Nothing more
than another silhouette on our shared horizon.
At night though, I've watched kids climb
that long cold corridor to the celestial,
the red glow of a cherry passed back and forth
between them like a single taillight winding its way
west down a late mountain road—pulsing, breaking,
another sharp turn on that half-moon landing—
those above having risen with such ease
over the rooftops and steeples, the switchbacks
of the Cumberland no longer obscured
by hackberries and fog, the dim illuminations
of billboards no longer hovering overhead
like messages from the future. I often think
of returning to that high vantage point,

have stood at its base and planned my climb—
daylight not yet flickered out like a bulb, stars
waiting to tend their signal fires. But I always
turn away and return the way I've come.
I already know how darkness folds over us,
the fear that comes with hard wind and rain.
I already know how slowly exhaust lifts
from the industrial yards, that switchboard
of boulevards and overpasses I come from
pressed like an ember in the amber
of its own light and so certain of its being.

THE YEAR HYAKATUKE WAS SAID

Comet Hyakutake, formally designated C/1996 B2, was discovered on January 31, 1996. Dubbed "The Great Comet of 1996," its passage near the Earth was one of the closest cometary approaches in recorded history.

The year Hyakatuke was said
to strike the earth, I was in love
with Lauren Orr, the girl I watched crosscourt
at the homecoming game—her school
our rival—and who I believed watched me despite
the close contest—a foul, a free throw,
a buzzer beater—Lauren
a dancer with short, even blond hair
and who wore that night
a blue, floral-print blouse I still like to imagine
she slept in, thinking of me
as the delicately stenciled violets
branched up from her sleep,
their heart-shaped foliage spreading wild, Venus
unfolding from the crests of curtains
like waves with the wind through the windows
of her small white bedroom
in her small white house with its sloped
green roof and cool, yellow glow.

I first heard of Hyakatuke a week later
as I walked the wide hallways between German
and trigonometry, mouthing the words
Ich liebe dich, I love you, Ich liebe dich,
in love with a girl for the first time
and suddenly vision of that halo-winged coma
of white-hot gas, the core a pupil widening

47

on the horizon, that angry eye of iridium and ice
streaking in on its fuzzed spectrum of light
having swung by for so long on its innocent
elliptical through the solar system.

I wanted to run, make something
of that orbit I wore in the brick-red track
of recycled tractor-trailer tires—
fifty seconds per loop, four-and-a-quarter minutes
per mile—track meet after track meet
my name pressed in thin columns of print
on the last of the sports pages on Sundays,
her school named after the man who wrote "Letter
From Birmingham Jail"
three miles uphill past barrel fires
and men circled around them,
the bits of glass I picked from the soles
of my Nikes turning my fingers red
before I turned back in a sprint downhill,
calves saddled to my legs and I riding them
wherever they would take me.

Since, I've not known such heat.
Have not been pressed beneath such extinguishing
fire: landlocked by hall monitors, "College Application:
Pending," conjugating German modals: *Ich liebe,*
du liebst, er, sie, es liebt, in one mind,
and in the other, the mountain
I often dreamed of: a perfect green isosceles,
blue veins of rivulets swiveling down to the foothills,
woodsmoke in wisps from the stovepipes
of a few cottages as, above it all,
Hyakatuke draws a bead, its bright white iris
widened to the polished skull of a ghost hare

returned for blood, Lauren and I atop that apogee
as the seas boil over and earth's core retracts,
great steamed jetties blasting solarward
from the evaporated poles,
our bodies spiraling upward to the heavens,
light of our cells *flash flash flash,* vaporized,
great plumes of smoke rising,
the American elms that lined my street
bursting into bright red asters, the wobbly
machinery of the moon dropping
toward the bleary square of light that shone
from the basement window, its splash glow
articulating the laces of our sneakers
as we listened to the sound of her father
between notes. The piano. All that sound.
The chords drifting upward and out
into nowhere.

DRIVING INTO THE CUMBERLAND

for Peter Wyatt

They know they aren't the first or the last, clanging along
in their clambake of 30-weight and redlined RPMs, blood brothers
weaving in and out of the US-100's metered yellow dashes.
They're sixteen making their way fifteen miles west of town
to that sheer drop of Tennessee limestone where, gas pedal
weighed down with a cinderblock and stick-shifted into *D*,
they watch that V-6 peel out in a sidewinder of mud clods

and black exhaust to somersault eighty feet to the Cheatham
County Cumberland below. These are the days before death
and finances will stop them back at the fork in the highway,
the days when they still compare the putting on of a condom
to suiting up for the moon and are angry at their fathers
for being their fathers. When they think back on it,
they'll think it's all the unknowing of sixteen years that drove

them to that promontory, the Continental's single headlamp
coppering as it sank like a submersible in the waters made murky
by runoff, to watch it disappear around a bend in the river
and know for fact they've left their mark on the city of their births,
to peer into the shallows of the riverfront eight blocks
from their high school and envision that Continental at rest
in that mausoleum of Cutlass Sierras and totaled GTOs.

What was it about that Continental that just begged to fly? they'll ask
all summer, rewriting the details of their story beyond even their own
disbelief. Just watch how, electing to stay in the car, they toss back
the last dregs of their fifth of tequila, yell *Fuck it!* and floor
that once luxury four-door, speeding for the cliff's edge. What song
Billy Corgan chirrs through the radio will change hands in the telling
innumerable times. What degree of fullness the moon, they will

be wise to misremember. Look at them, swimming by its baleful light back to shore. Look at them lying and laughing together. Tonight they are alive. Tonight they are breathing. Neither is thinking of the long walk home. Neither yet knows that weaving their way back to town through the moonlit dark, that stumbling stoned along the edge of the highway they just drove, Peter will keep saying, *Look, it's the world. We're finally seeing the world.*

SELF-PORTRAIT AT 5 A.M.

First light, and the starlings name themselves one
by one, wind swelling like an ocean, leaf to dagger-
pointed leaf through the willow. Everything but me
seems to have its instruction: the hare shuffling
through the brush to its burrow, no-see-ums rising
in mute droves, each slat of the venetian blinds
an intonation of light. But this is where I keep my allegiances,
in this room of no sleep so thick with silence it claims
its own configuration: that thin cord of luminance
beneath my bedroom door a stropped edge of steel,
the image the window holds most clear when I look through it,
my face afloat in the glass—yet another false image
imposed on my backyard, yet another false image
floating freely on the reflection of the waking world.

NIGHTSWIM

New growth budding on the May
month trees, we troll our rail thin bodies
        through the waters of Nathan Hansen's pool—
his mother and father out for the night
and it only logical our clothes shucked
        poolside in the grass as the first
        evening bats emerge to wing their scripture
across the holy eyes of planets.

It's as if we are subjects in a grand
experiment: Nathan, Joanna, and I sprinting naked
        in turn the narrow tongue of the board
        and crying out distantly between the twangs
of our dives and our splashdowns—
        lean and pale as the stripped spines of feathers.
        Together, we wade beneath that giant lens of sky,
all three of us expert in our virgining,

        the light through the hardwoods that hangs
above the pool painting us one shade
        lighter than the dark, the flick of our bodies
        like newborn spirits gravestone to gravestone,
the white rinds of our smiling mouths
        streak-lines in a mirror. And perhaps
        I should credit dumb luck, perhaps instinct, when
thinking our backs are turned, Joanna rises

        to perch but a moment on the pool's
concrete cuff, and watching water slide from her back
        like mercury laved from a larger body of mercury,

I reach for the globe of the sheepdog's
tennis ball and thrust it, ask anyone,
    striking one of those ill-fated bats
  midflight. Stunned, it tumbles like a fletchless
arrow shot straight for the center

  of the earth, but by the time
it should have smacked down in the water,
    we no longer can see it, that tiny
  creature an agent of night
and even the last paring of moon occluded
    in that pin's drop of time when the bat
  must have snapped out of its dream
and opened its wings as dark as dark

  hibiscus blooms. The one thing
we *can* see is that blade of liquid drawn
    when its wing skims the pool's
  meniscus. The one thing we can make out is Joanna
at the pool's edge, still for once
    in the trick light of the corner
  of the eye. The night naked and quiet.
The shudder of water rippling silently around us.

PERSEUS

for Judy Jordan

No words for that which holds him here so silent:
mortal on this limestone bluff, wet leaves dead
beneath wet snow and day's last light scouring
the west face of the ridge. Last night,

it was the comet he eyed through the lens: elusive,
walleyed luminance swelled between the crosshairs. Now,
late dusk, it's an answer he seeks of the upcountry,
of its rivers carved long ago by glaciers. Now,

it's an answer he seeks of this stunned earth, of this
stunned body—body bound to nickel, body bound
to iron—body bound by the selfsame forces
that fix Perseus in the high north sky. But he doubts

he's as alone as this arrangement of stars, the screech
owl's wail descending through the night, the bobcat's cry
to the sun-turned-moon—all of us with this need

for some belief, with this need for some faith.
That someplace deep: a fire-blazoned core. That someplace
not far: an ear for such lost and lonely music.

LOST CREEK CAVE

First, travel east seventy-plus miles from my home,
then wait for the telltale fog to rise from the banks
of the Caney Fork which snakes beneath I-40
six times in six miles. Turn south. Follow the Kill Calf tributary
to a town so small one year it's called Star City—
Three Eagles' Crossing the next.

Now travel ten years into the past. Track the coos
of mourning doves you once believed were owls
retired in the transom of the mulberry treetops.
Listen, hand cupped to ear, for the scamper of squirrels
up the pale-necked sycamores. Look east for the sun
as it releases its ballast to rise above the pines:
helix snails feelering from the underside of dawn
and the talons of night stalkers clicking shut as field mice
and voles squabble for seed, the basin of the Star City Sink
dished like a crater in the dense landscape.

Shade your eyes and you'll find us: John and my father,
best friends, and Peter and me, side by side
before the crooked black spiracle of the cave, a gold disc
of light strapped to my forehead as the dim blue vein
of Lost Creek cascades from the rim at our backs,
scoops from the Tennessee bedrock the swimming hole
we dog-paddled those summers despite the inward tug
of its waters—Lost Creek slipping those secret
causeways into the earth.
                    Lost.

        * * *

56

My father's telling consults the map, one of many
he framed to the kitchen's sheetrock with strips of trim
and a few tacking nails: Tennessee a parallelogram,
Mill Creek and the Little Harpeth and all the other
trout streams we anglered felt-tipped to wrinkled paper,
an X scrawled to note the highest peak of the Smokies,
Lost Creek Cave a circle drawn in my father's hand
to the dead center of White County, there beneath,

where water stands in pools so clear it seems suitable
only for the holy, there beneath where miles of rim pools
are sculpted by earth drip and acres of onyx branch down
from low ceilings, our only light the quicksilver beams
of our halogens as we belly these opaline flows of stone—
hands and knees along these chines and sluices,
grooves in rock like whorls worked into wood.

    * * *

This is a story we tell together, father and son,
most recently at my sister's wedding where I watched
him walk her down the aisle we fashioned
from borrowed folding chairs in her backyard,
the two of us in her kitchen a little bit later and a little bit drunk
as my father conjured Lost Creek Cave before us,

     Which curves beneath itself
                like a ram's horn,

he says, drawing the spiral of a corkscrew in midair,
the cave's perfect center now balanced on my father's fingertip
where silver sheets of water spill from the stone firmament
like rain through a buckshot tin roof, and where John, Peter,
my father and I approach that dark waterfall,
our reflections fluttering like hummingbird wings in its waters—

Each of us seeking from that blackness another self?
Each of us a beacon?
Each of us a gold nimbus of fire?

　　* * *

Now it seems obvious to my father:
the cave bats tucked into the heights, driftwood the size of caskets
smoothed down to their alluvials, countless skulls
of wild boar and deer antlers scattered like offerings
on high shelves of stone.

But how we could have known three storms
met that afternoon above White County, I do not know.

　　　　There is something within us, I say,

　　　　Some other sense, my father adds,

when wriggling miles deep through a squeeze in the cave,
my headlamp blinked out and everything went quiet.
Fumbling with my lighter, it was as though I'd dropped
into the hollow skirt of a bell. The earth thumping its chest
like the first shovelfuls of soil on a grave, I was thrust into the spark
of steel and white gas, thumb singed by the spool of burning flint,

and I heard a sound like the sound of stone against stone,
a rush like diving off a lake dock in the middle of the night,
a sound like the sound of all the old laws flooding back,
the tablets drug by some mute creature across the cave bottom—
each chiseled syllable of God tapping out its code into stone as I,

scrambling backward through the crawlspace, felt along mica grooves
and instinct back through the squeeze through the dark
until, finally, I found them, John, Peter, and my father side

by side on a ledge overlooking the cave's main passage: the crest
and curve of whitewater rapids blocking the way home.

       * * *

But why would you do this? my uncle asks,
this the story of my father's near second death by water.

Why this life not a life without death's clang
from time to time between the ears?

No one knows what holds the balances:
    why our children don't float too deep into their dreams,
    why the Mississippi floods each spring to feed the farmlands,
    why drawbridges don't collapse on the bows of mother ships.

Who is it out there
twirling the earth like a basketball on a fingertip?

       * * *

This time there is no darkness.
This time we're in my sister's kitchen, the redolence
of coffee drifting by in dust motes. This time
our lives are certain—no echo, no water—just my father and me
surrounded by family and wedding guests: my sister
in her beaded gown, he in his fitted tux. This time
the late May sun slants through my sister's kitchen windows
to splash across us in glazed right angles of light,

and it's just my father and me who link arms
and step out into the flooded cave passage
and are swept upward and back by the surge,
my father indicating the water's height with the edge of his palm
at times as high as his chest, me leaning forward like a sprinter

sprung from the blocks—this a story
I dare not tell without my father, fearful
we'll be sucked back into that earth and will slip back
into that place of black water, of siege and surge, of *echo*
echo echo—fearful that this time, disoriented,
we'll allow that rare river to tow us back to the waterfall
which will part its curtains before us,

and this time we'll see our doubles, our dream selves just beyond:
John, Peter, my father and I gesturing *Come,*
Come as we march forward, linked at the arms like metal links of chain,
my father shuffling to keep his footing, and me crying out

Keep moving! Keep moving!

this the only sound above the rip of rapids
as we become lost forever in those dark wakes.

                    * * *

My father's favorite part of the story is how,
when light finally broke around a bend in the cave,
he turned to look at me and saw me for the first time.

Sometimes I wonder if we're not still there: John, Peter,
my father and I: waterlogged, exhausted, jubilant,
the flooded cave entrance a whisper at our backs.
Peter, my best friend who I met on the front steps
of kindergarten, Peter, my best man, nearly homeless
on his twenty-third birthday. Peter who now has a child.
John, whose hair turned brown to silver by the age of thirty.
John whose daughter leapt ten years ago from a building.
My father who plants a garden each spring: tomatoes,
a row of basil, greens, three for corn, green pole beans
planted at their feet to scale sunward the yellow-and-white

cobbed stalks. My father who edges closer to his last days.
And I who ask you to take my hand like the seeds I poured
from their paper pouch and tucked in rows into April's
slowly warming matter. I who promise to protect you,
to bring you out if you will promise to enter, Lost Creek Cave
a serpentine of water streaming in from the north
like a string trailing after its balloon battered in the wind.

Put this poem down, I ask.
Let it float like an ark on sleeping waters.

Stand up. Close your eyes. Take a step forward.

Imagine you are walking through water.

FIRST CATCH

First light, and the moon rises in the west,
all the rivers and creeks and streams racing in opposite directions,
the freshwater clams dart-clapping forward

and the seventeen-year cicadas burrowing deeper
as the mother robins recall their sermons through the willow groves
and all the blue-egg bird shells reconstruct, and we all

become children again: Mary's body lifting
from the pavement to ascend the seven stories to the rooftop
she leapt from the year I turned drinking age,

David Cross's fists pulling back and all the blood I lost
in the seventh grade flinging back into my nostrils
like red serpents charmed by the sweet music of flutes,

baseball rising from the zoysia grass just beyond left center
and racing back through the sky, back into my hand and again
we are one pitch away from being crowned champions

as I stand on this creek bed, a yogurt container of worms and dirt
at my feet, this rainbow trout the first catch of my life
gulping in my hands for air, and soon enough its belly slit

from tail to gills, its innards of bruise-blue mollusk shells
and grit thumbed loose from the meat most succulent when brushed
with olive oil and packed in salt beneath the broiler's blue coil.

      * * *

Give this body a voice, and aloud I'll say death.
Give this voice a body, and I'll drop to my knees, rub my face raw
with the river stones of rivers and ask for forgiveness.

But words are merely words, this flash and ebb
of Mill Creek no more than a trick of memories and light
as I sit here, having risen yet again before dawn

to write this scene and rewrite this scene
in which I am just a boy sitting with his back to the cutbank
playing his hands through air: first emulating beech trees

tossed about in the wind, then flocks in their fleets
from white-ash contrail to white-ash contrail, finally a figure
descending to the swift water's edge where,

weightless, it lifts from the earth and I too am lifted,
carried out across the city of my birth that transforms before me
from dilapidated 7-Elevens and U-turns and acid rain

into fields of tobacco and shimmering silos and rays of sun
as I follow the sliver of concrete and paint known as Route 9
all the way back to the Mill Creek I remember,

where, this time, I ease the buck knife shut and,
with a precision like language, remove the hook
from the lip of my first trout, this time

I return this first catch of my life to the chill
and together, my father and I watch as it fins back
into darkness and again we find ourselves moving in reverse:

hooked worm zipping back along its half-dome
of microfilament, my rod relaxed, the iron lattices
and girders of the concrete bridge under which we cast our lines

ripping from their footings as Route 9's aggregate
of asphalt and tar evaporates into the atmosphere
and all the beasts yoked to their wagonloads moving west

through the Appalachians buckle to their knees—
no settlers ever staking a claim to Nolensville, Tennessee,
Mill Creek forever untouched, and I never born.

        * * *

But what about you? You who've watched me
unpack this trout from ice. You who've watched me watch
my father dip it in buttermilk, roll it in a shallow bowl

of cornmeal—that silent beaded eye turning over to its white.
You who may be the caster of iron beams: *What did that fish
first see when I pulled it from water?* You

who may be one of the undocumented who stuffed my walls
with pink scurls of insulation and leveled the concrete slab:
Of what do fish dream? What dreams did I cease?

You who know how to rub the string of pearls back down
to a handful of sand. You who know the backwards skitter
of fire. You? You were never here.